BOOK 3 - Eb Alto Saxophone

STANDARD OF EXCELLENCE

COMPREHENSIVE BAND METHOD

By Bruce Pearson

Dear Student:

Welcome to STANDARD OF EXCELLENCE Book 3.

By now, you have demonstrated that you are making steady progress toward becoming an accomplished musician. With the skills you are mastering on your instrument, you are beginning to realize the value of hard work and the joy of music-making.

STANDARD OF EXCELLENCE Book 3 introduces you to some of the world's finest music. By performing this literature, you will gain an appreciation for a variety of musical styles while improving your individual instrument and ensemble skills.

Best wishes as you explore Book 3.

Sincerely,

Bruce Pearson

Practicing - the key to EXCELLENCE!

▶ Make practicing part of your daily schedule. If you plan it as you do any other activity, you will find plenty of time for it.

▶ Try to practice in the same place every day. Choose a place where you can concentrate on making music. Start with a regular and familiar warm-up routine, including long tones and simple technical exercises. Like an athlete, you need to warm-up your mind and muscles before you begin performing.

▶ Set goals for every practice session. Keep track of your practice time and progress on the front cover Practice Journal.

▶ Practice the hard spots in your lesson assignments and band music over and over, until you can play them perfectly.

▶ At the end of each practice session, play something fun.

ISBN 0-8497-5981-1

kjos NEIL A. KJOS MUSIC COMPANY, PUBLISHER

2

REVIEW	G MAJOR KEY SIGNATURE	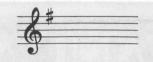
STYLE	*simile* - Continue playing in the same manner.	

1 WARM-UP - Band Arrangement

Andante

▶ Plan where to take breaths.

2 TECHNIQUE BREAK

Moderato

simile

3 RIG A JIG JIG

American Folk Song

Moderato

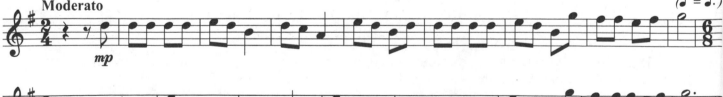

4 TECHNIQUE BREAK

Allegretto

simile

▶ *Use the alternate F♯/G♭ fingering.

REVIEW	E MINOR KEY SIGNATURE	

5 E MINOR SCALE SKILL (Concert G Minor)

6 PAT-A-PAN

French Carol

7 INTERVAL INQUISITION

▶ Write in the intervals on the lines provided.

8 ARTICULATION ADVENTURE

9 GO FOR EXCELLENCE!

▶ Lines with a medal are *Achievement Lines.* The chart on the inside back cover can be used to record your progress.

4

REVIEW	C MAJOR KEY SIGNATURE	

10 DYNAMIC DYNAMICS

Andante

pp ———————————— ff ———————————— pp

11 MAJOR AND MINOR CHORD EAR TRAINER

Major Chord   div.   unis.   div.   Minor Chord   unis.   div.

1 3 1 5 1 3 5 3 1   1 3 1 5 1 3 5 3 1

▶ Sing before you play.

12 TECHNIQUE BREAK

Moderato
mp   mf
ff   mf
1.   2.
pp   pp

13 MY PARTNER AND I

Swedish Folk Dance

Allegretto
div.
mf
f   mf
f

14 FOR ALTO SAXOPHONES ONLY

Page 44 ▶

Moderato C#   D
mf

▶ When you see a page number followed by an arrow, *Excellerate* to the page indicated for additional studies.

W23XE

REVIEW | **D MAJOR KEY SIGNATURE**

20 WARM-UP - Band Arrangement

Andante

21 TECHNIQUE BREAK

Moderato

22 THE BRITISH GRENADIERS

English Folk Song

Maestoso

▶ Try to breathe only at the end of phrases.

23 FOR ALTO SAXOPHONES ONLY

Andante

W23XE

REVIEW

A MAJOR KEY SIGNATURE

SIXTEENTH/ DOTTED EIGHTH NOTE COMBINATION

ENHARMONICS

A# = Bb

24 A MAJOR SCALE SKILL (Concert C Major)

Moderato
Arpeggio
Chords div.
mf

25 ARTICULATION ADVENTURE

Andante
mf

clap

▶ Write in the counting for the top line before you play.

26 GREEN GROW THE RASHES O

Scottish Folk Song

Moderato
mf

A#

27 TECHNIQUE BREAK

Andante
mf

28 GO FOR EXCELLENCE!

Scottish Folk Song

Andante
"Bonnie Glen Shee"
mp

REVIEW	F MAJOR KEY SIGNATURE	

| SIXTEENTH/EIGHTH/ SIXTEENTH NOTE COMBINATION |  | 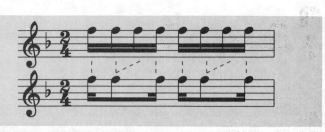 |

29 F MAJOR SCALE SKILL (Concert A♭ Major) Page 44 ▬▬▶

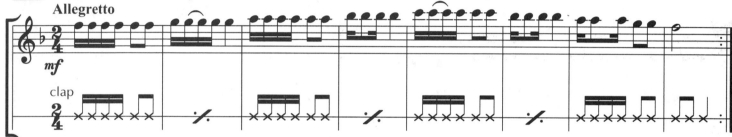

▶ Try playing both octaves.

30 ARTICULATION ADVENTURE

▶ Write in the counting for the top line before you play.

31 LA RASPA

Mexican Folk Song

32 TECHNIQUE BREAK

Andante

▶ Try playing both octaves.

10

B MINOR KEY SIGNATURE	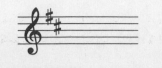	**B minor** has the same key signature as **D major**.
TEMPO		**Andantino** - Faster than **Andante**, but not as fast as **Moderato**.

38 WARM-UP - Band Arrangement

39 B MINOR SCALE SKILL (Concert D Minor)

▶ Try playing both octaves.

40 TECHNIQUE BREAK

▶ * Use the alternate F# fingering.

41 FOR ALTO SAXOPHONES ONLY

▶ * Use the alternate F fingering.

W23XF

SIXTEENTH REST

γ = ¼ count in $\frac{2}{4}$, $\frac{3}{4}$, and $\frac{4}{4}$ time.

A sixteenth rest is as long as a sixteenth note.

42 TINGA LAYO   Page 44 ▶   West Indies Folk Song

Moderato

div.

mf

Fine

D.C. al Fine

© M. Baron Co. Used by permission.

43 HWI NE YA HE   American Indian Song

Allegro

f

44 SIXTEENTH STUDY

Andantino

A   B   C

mf

D   E   F

▶ Write in the counting and clap the rhythm before you play.

45 GO FOR EXCELLENCE!   French Canadian Folk Song

Allegretto

"Envoyons D'L'Avant, Nos Gens!"

mp

▶ Name the key in "Go For Excellence!"_____

DOTTED QUARTER REST

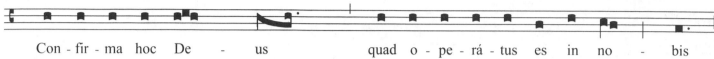
A dot after a rest adds half the value of the rest.

46 CONFIRMA HOC

Plainsong

Con - fir - ma hoc De - us   quad o - pe - rá - tus es in no - bis

▶ Keep the eighth notes even at all times.
© G.I.A. Publications, Inc. Used by permission.

47 DESCENDIT DE COELIS

Notre Dame Organum

48 ESTAMPIE

Anonymous

49 SUMER IS ICUMEN IN

English Round

W23XE

THE RENAISSANCE (1400 - 1600)

Bb MAJOR KEY SIGNATURE

This key signature means play all B's as B flats and all E's as E flats.

50 Bb MAJOR SCALE SKILL (Concert Db Major)
Page 44

► Try playing both octaves.

51 VOX DILECTI MEI - Band Arrangement

Palestrina (1525 - 1594)
arr. Bruce Pearson (b. 1942)

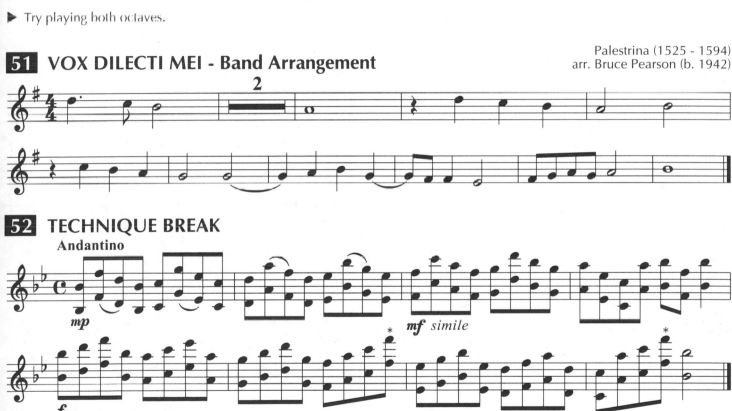

52 TECHNIQUE BREAK

► *Use the alternate high F fingering.
► Try playing both octaves.

53 GO FOR EXCELLENCE!

Thoinot Arbeau (1520 - 1595)

"The Official Branle"

THE RENAISSANCE, continued

54 OLD ONE HUNDREDTH - Band Arrangement

Louis Bourgeois (c. 1510 - c. 1561)
arr. Bruce Pearson (b. 1942)

55 NOW IS THE MONTH OF MAYING

Thomas Morley (1557 - 1602)

56 TECHNIQUE BREAK Page 45 ▶

Allegro

simile

57 BERGERETTE SANS ROCHE

Basse Danse
Tielman Susato (c. 1500 - c. 1561)

▶ Try playing both octaves.

58 FOR ALTO SAXOPHONES ONLY

▶ Start slowly and increase speed.

EARLE OF OXFORDS MARCHE

Band Arrangement

William Byrd (1543 - 1623)
arr. Bruce Pearson (b. 1942)

59 _____ Arranger _____

your name

▶ Create fauxbourdon by writing a duet part a sixth below this Renaissance melody. Title your composition, and play the top part while a friend plays the bottom part.

60 GO FOR EXCELLENCE!

THE BAROQUE PERIOD (1600 - 1750)

| TRILL | | A rapid alternation from the written note to the note above it in the key of the piece. |

61 BALANCE BUILDER

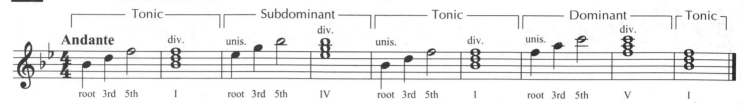

62 TRUMPET TUNE

Henry Purcell (1659 - 1695)

63 LE PETIT RIEN

François Couperin (1668 - 1733)

▶ When you see a staccato note at the end of a slur, slur to the note but make it short.

64 FOR ALTO SAXOPHONES ONLY   Page 45 ▶

▶ On the trills, move the key(s) as rapidly as possible. Keep the air moving.
▶ *Use the trill fingering found on page 47.

TIME SIGNATURE

$\frac{9}{8}$

9 = 9 counts in each measure
8 = eighth note gets 1 count

STYLE

grazioso - gracefully

65 TECHNIQUE BREAK

Allegretto

mf
grazioso

▶ Write in the counting and clap the rhythm before you play.

66 ALLEMANDE

Arcangelo Corelli (1653 - 1713)

Moderato

mf

rit. - 2nd time

67 THE FOUR SEASONS

Antonio Vivaldi (1678 - 1741)

Moderato

div.

f

1. *p*   2. *f*

1. *trm*   2.

rit. - 2nd time   *p*

68 GO FOR EXCELLENCE!

Johann Sebastian Bach (1685 - 1750)

Moderato

"Jesu, Joy of Man's Desiring"

mp *grazioso*

rit.

THE BAROQUE PERIOD, continued

69 CHORALE - Band Arrangement

Hans Leo Hassler (c. 1562 - 1612)
arr. Bruce Pearson (b. 1942)

70 HORNPIPE FROM "WATER MUSIC SUITE"

George Frideric Handel (1685 - 1759)

71 TECHNIQUE BREAK   Page 45 ▶

72 FANTASIA CHROMATICA

Johann Sebastian Bach (1685 - 1750)

▶ Try playing both octaves.

73 FOR ALTO SAXOPHONES ONLY

▶ Roll your thumb to and from the octave key.

SIXTEENTH NOTES IN 3/8, 6/8, & 9/8 TIME

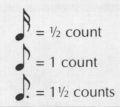

♪ = ½ count
♪ = 1 count
♪. = 1½ counts

A single sixteenth note is half as long as an eighth note.

74 ARTICULATION ADVENTURE

Moderato

mf

▶ Write in the counting and clap the rhythm before you play.

75 MINUETTO

Domenico Scarlatti (1685 - 1757)

Allegretto

▶ *cresc.* (<) - gradually play louder. *decresc.* (>) - gradually play softer.

76 PASSEPIED

Georg Philipp Telemann (1681 - 1767)

Allegro

© Southern Music Co. Used by permission.

77 GO FOR EXCELLENCE!

George Frideric Handel (1685 - 1759)

Andantino

"Siciliana from Music for the Royal Fireworks"

78 TECHNIQUE BREAK

▶ Name the key in "Technique Break." _____

REJOUISSANCE
from Music for the Royal Fireworks
Band Arrangement

George Frideric Handel (1685 - 1759)
arr. Bruce Pearson (b. 1942)

THE CLASSICAL PERIOD (1750-1820)

GRACE NOTE	TEMPO	STYLE
A small-sized note played just before the note to which it is attached.	**Larghetto -** not as slow as **Largo**	*dolce* - sweetly

79 THEME FROM PIANO SONATA NO. 2 — Wolfgang Amadeus Mozart (1756 - 1791)

80 GERMAN DANCE Page 45 — Franz Joseph Haydn (1732 - 1809)

81 TECHNIQUE BREAK

82 GO FOR EXCELLENCE! — Ludwig van Beethoven (1770 - 1827)

THE CLASSICAL PERIOD, continued

BINARY FORM	AB	Music that has two different sections.

83 AUSTRIAN HYMN - Band Arrangement

Franz Joseph Haydn (1732 - 1809)
arr. Bruce Pearson (b. 1942)

Andante
mf legato
mp
f
mp

84 RUSSIAN FOLK SONG

Ludwig van Beethoven (1770 - 1827)

Allegro
Section A
f
p

Section B
f
p
f

85 TECHNIQUE BREAK

Andante
mf
accel. - 2nd time

▶ Try playing both octaves.

86 FOR ALTO SAXOPHONES ONLY

A   B   C   D

mf

▶ Play each pattern four times. Start slowly and increase speed.

| TERNARY FORM | ABA | The A section is followed by the B section, and then the A section is played again. |

87 SCOTCH DANCE   Page 45 ▐▐▐▐➤   Ludwig van Beethoven (1770 - 1827)

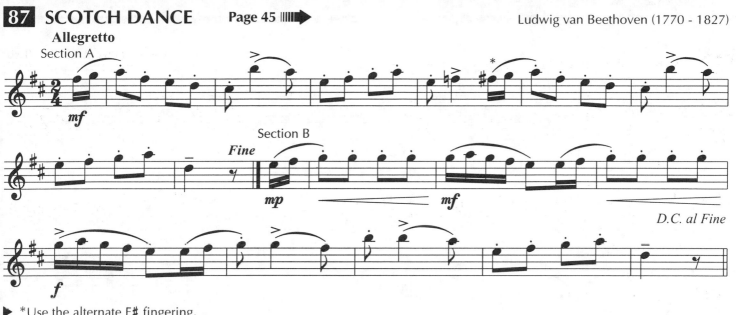

▶ *Use the alternate F# fingering.
▶ Name the form used in "Scotch Dance." _____

88 TECHNIQUE BREAK   Rodolphe Kreutzer (1766 - 1831)

89 GO FOR EXCELLENCE!   Wolfgang Amadeus Mozart (1756 - 1791)

*Use the alternate C fingering.

THE CLASSICAL PERIOD, continued

| RONDO FORM | ABACA | The main section A returns several times and alternates with other sections. |

90 **CADENCES**

RONDO
Band Arrangement

Franz Joseph Haydn (1732 - 1809)
arr. Bruce Pearson (b. 1942)

THE ROMANTIC PERIOD (1820 - 1900)

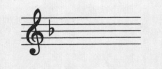

D MINOR KEY SIGNATURE

D minor has the same key signature as **F major**.

91 CAST THY BURDEN FROM "ELIJAH" - Band Arrangement
Felix Mendelssohn (1809 - 1847)
arr. Bruce Pearson (b. 1942)

92 D MINOR SCALE SKILL (Concert F Minor) Page 45

▶ Try playing both octaves.

93 TECHNIQUE BREAK

94 GO FOR EXCELLENCE!
Johannes Brahms (1833 - 1897)
"Hungarian Dance No. 5"

THE ROMANTIC PERIOD, continued

TIME SIGNATURE	$\frac{6}{4}$	**6** = 6 counts in each measure **4** = quarter note gets 1 count

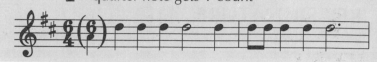

DAL SEGNO AL CODA (D.S. AL CODA)	Go back to the segno sign (𝄋) and play until the coda sign. When you reach the coda sign, skip to the *Coda.*

95 **SCHEHERAZADE**

Nicolai Rimsky-Korsakov (1844 - 1908)

96 **LAUGHING SONG FROM "DIE FLEDERMAUS"**

Johann Strauss, Jr. (1825 - 1899)

▶ Write in the counting and clap the rhythm before you play.

97 **FIRE FESTIVAL POLKA**

Josef Strauss (1827 - 1870)

98 **FOR ALTO SAXOPHONES ONLY**

TIME SIGNATURE 5/4

5 = 5 counts in each measure
4 = quarter note gets 1 count

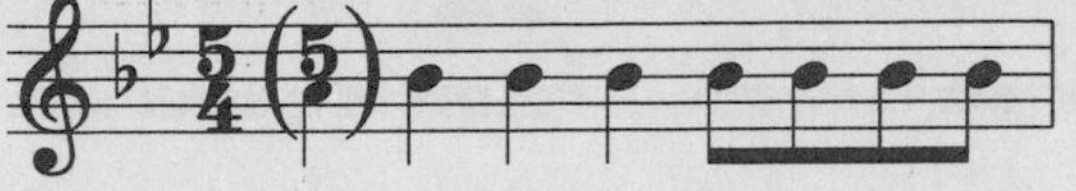

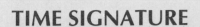

E MAJOR KEY SIGNATURE

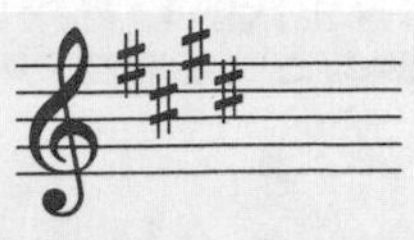

This key signature means play all F's as F sharps, all C's as C sharps, all G's as G sharps, and all D's as D sharps.

STYLE

sostenuto - sustained

99 TECHNIQUE BREAK

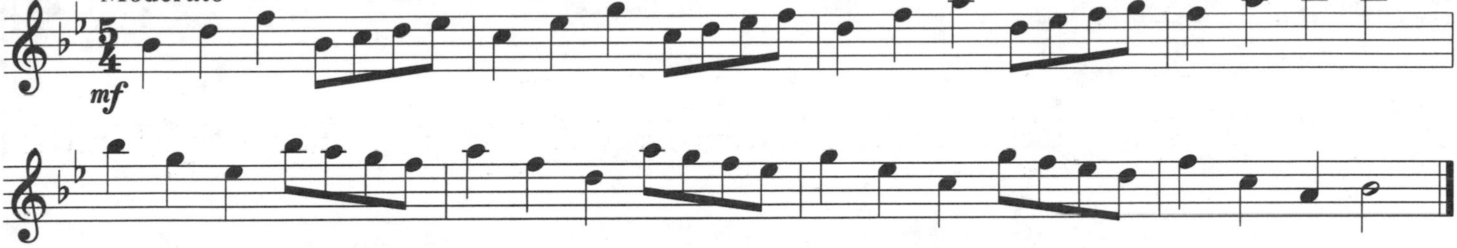
Moderato
mf

▶ Write in the counting and clap the rhythm before you play.

100 E MAJOR SCALE SKILL (Concert G Major)

Page 45

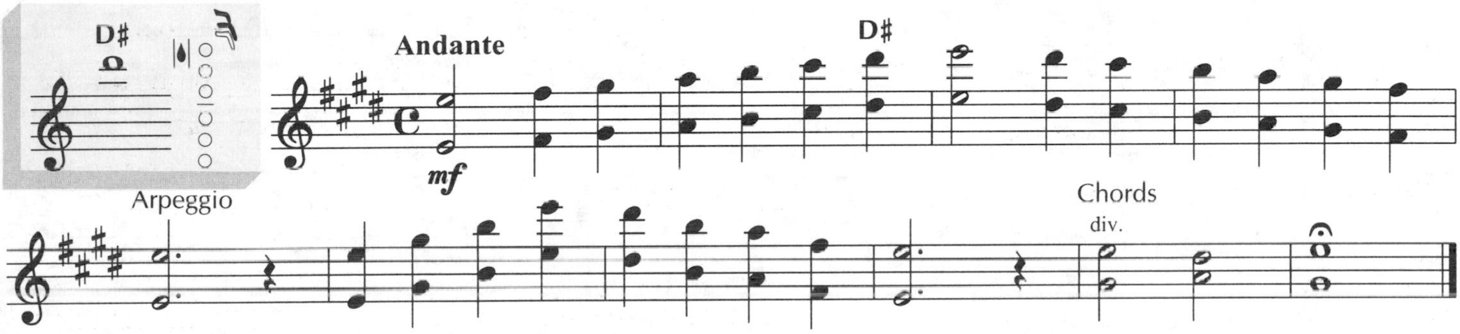
D♯
Andante
D♯
mf
Arpeggio
Chords
div.

▶ Try playing both octaves.

101 PILGRIMS CHORUS FROM "TANNHAUSER"

Richard Wagner (1813 - 1883)

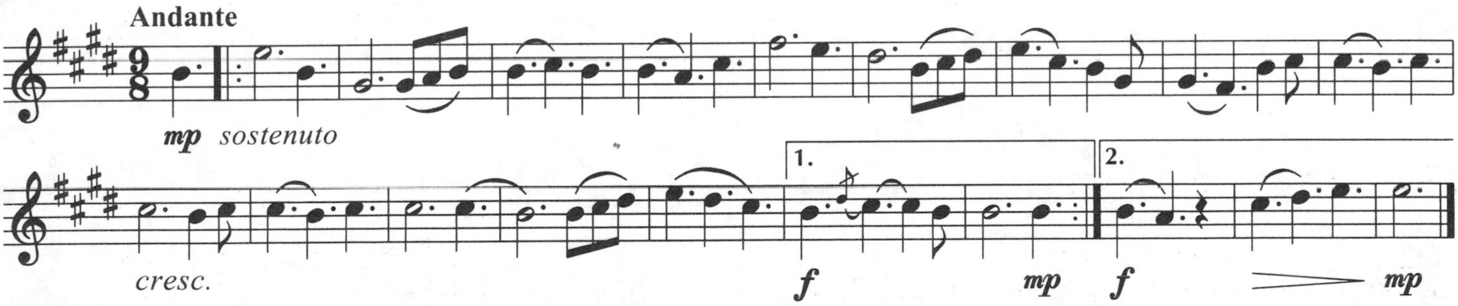
Andante
mp sostenuto
1.
2.
cresc.
f
mp
f
mp

102 GO FOR EXCELLENCE!

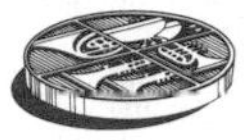

Modeste Mussorgsky (1839 - 1881)

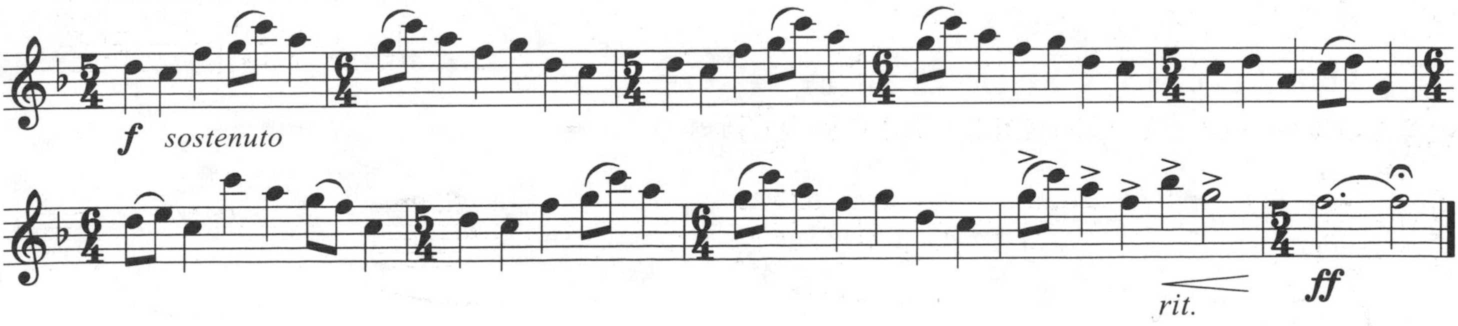
Maestoso
"Promenade from Pictures at an Exhibition"
f sostenuto
rit.
ff

28

THE ROMANTIC PERIOD, continued

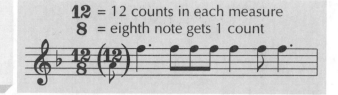

TIME SIGNATURE	$\frac{12}{8}$	**12** = 12 counts in each measure **8** = eighth note gets 1 count	DYNAMICS

sforzando (sfz) - accented

103 ARTICULATION ADVENTURE

▶ Write in the counting and clap the rhythm before you play.

104 TECHNIQUE BREAK

Carl Czerny (1791 - 1857)

105 THE WILD HORSEMAN

Robert Schumann (1810 - 1856)

▶ Line A is in the key of E minor (concert G minor). On line B, write in the melody a whole step lower to transpose to the key of D minor (concert F minor). Play both lines.

106 FOR ALTO SAXOPHONES ONLY

▶ * Use the alternate C fingering.

W23XE

STYLE

cantabile -
in a singing style

ENHARMONICS

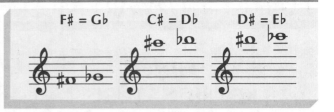

F♯ = G♭   C♯ = D♭   D♯ = E♭

WALTZ
from Waltz Op. 39, No. 15
Band Arrangement

Johannes Brahms (1833 - 1897)
arr. Chris Salerno (b. 1968)

107 TECHNIQUE BREAK

▶ *Use the alternate F♯/G♭ fingerings.
▶ Try playing both octaves.

108 GO FOR EXCELLENCE!

Peter Ilyich Tchaikovsky (1840 - 1893)

Andante
"Theme from Symphony No. 5"

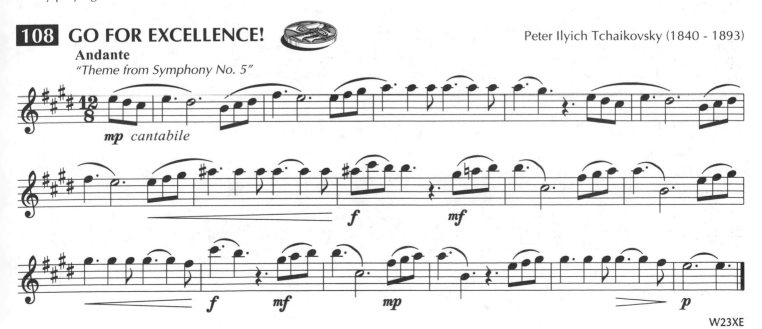

20th CENTURY ART MUSIC

F♯ MINOR KEY SIGNATURE

F♯ **minor** has the same key signature as **A major.**

ENHARMONICS

E♯ = F

---

109 **F♯ MINOR SCALE SKILL (Concert A Minor)**   Page 45 ▶

Page 45 ▶

Moderato

Natural Minor   Harmonic Minor   E♯

Melodic Minor   Arpeggio   Chords div.

110 **PAVANE**   Gabriel Fauré (1845 - 1924)

Andantino

mp cantabile

▶ *Use the alternate F♯ fingering.

111 **WHOLE-TONE SCALE STUDY**

Andante

mf

▶ A whole-tone scale consists of only whole steps.

112 **EXCERPT FROM "PRELUDE TO THE AFTERNOON OF A FAUN"**

Impressionism Example
Claude Debussy (1862 - 1918)

Moderato

p —— *mp* —— *p* —— *mp*

▶ This piece is based on a whole-tone scale. In measure 6, be sure to trill up a whole step.

113 **THE SUNKEN CATHEDRAL - Band Arrangement**

Impressionism Example
Claude Debussy (1862 - 1918)
arr. Chuck Elledge (b. 1961)

Maestoso

ff

▶ This piece demonstrates a technique called planing, where all notes of a chord move the same direction. This is also called parallel motion.

ASYMMETRICAL METERS

Meters or time signatures with an uneven number of eighth notes (usually $\frac{3}{8}$, $\frac{5}{8}$, or $\frac{7}{8}$).

114 FOLK MELODY A LA BÉLA BARTÓK (1881 - 1945)

Nationalism Example
Stephen Foster (1826 - 1864)
arr. Chris Salerno (b. 1968)

Allegretto
"Oh! Susanna"

115 ODE TO IGOR STRAVINSKY (1882 - 1971) - **Band Arrangement**

Primitivism Example
Chris Salerno (b. 1968)

Moderato

116 TECHNIQUE BREAK

Moderato

▶ Write in the counting and clap the rhythm before you play.

117 GO FOR EXCELLENCE!

Claude Debussy (1862 - 1918)

Allegro
"Golliwog's Cake Walk from Children's Corner"

20TH CENTURY ART MUSIC, continued

DYNAMICS

forte-piano (***fp***) - loud, then immediately soft

ENHARMONICS

Twelve-tone Example
Chris Salerno (b. 1968)

118 **HOMAGE TO ANTON WEBERN (1883 - 1945)**

Tone Row

▶ Notice that the tone row uses all twelve notes of the chromatic scale once.

Moderato

119 **TONE ROW**   Page 46 ▶

Moderato

120 _____   Composer _____

your name

▶ Compose a twelve-tone composition. Title and play your composition.

121 **FOR ALTO SAXOPHONES ONLY**   Page 46 ▶

Andante   Db

WAR
from The Four Horsemen
Band Arrangement

Andrew Boysen, Jr. (b. 1968)

122 TRIBUTE TO CHARLES IVES (1874 - 1954)

Bitonal Example
Stephen Foster (1826 - 1864)
arr. Chris Salerno (b. 1968)

Allegretto

"Camptown Races"

123 GO FOR EXCELLENCE!

Moderato

▶ *Use the alternate F♯ fingering.

20th CENTURY POP MUSIC

Page 46

► Write in the counting and clap the rhythm before you play.

STYLE

Swing - ♪♪ played as ♪³♪

TWO-MEASURE REPEAT SIGN

Repeat the two previous measures.

128 SWINGING BLUES SCALE

129 SWINGING BLUES CHORD PROGRESSION (Arpeggios)

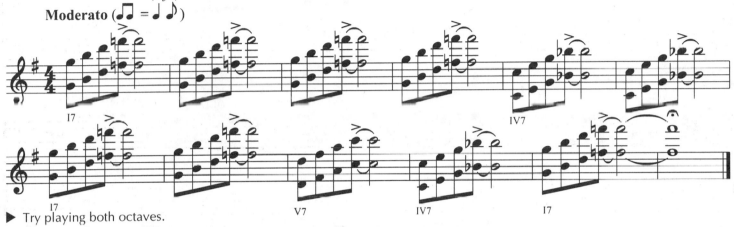

▶ Try playing both octaves.

130 BLUES CHORD ACCOMPANIMENT - Band Arrangement

▶ This exercise can be played with 131 and 132.

131 TIN ROOF BLUES   Page 46 ◀▶   Traditional Blues Example

132 GO FOR EXCELLENCE!

"Blues for a Fat Cat"

W23XE

20th Century Pop Music, continued

133 '55 T-BIRD

1950s Rock and Roll Example
Kevin Daley (b. 1957)

134 RIGHT ON

1970s Rock Example
Kevin Daley (b. 1957)

▶ Write in the counting and clap the rhythm before you play.

JAMBALAYA JAMMIN'
Band Arrangement

James "Red" McLeod (b. 1912)

W23XE

SCALE STUDIES

1 **G MAJOR SCALE (Concert B♭ Major)**

2 **E HARMONIC MINOR SCALE (Concert G Harmonic Minor)**

3 **C MAJOR SCALE (Concert E♭ Major)**

4 **A HARMONIC MINOR SCALE (Concert C Harmonic Minor)**

SCALE STUDIES

5 **D MAJOR SCALE (Concert F Major)**

6 **B HARMONIC MINOR SCALE (Concert D Harmonic Minor)**

7 **F MAJOR SCALE (Concert A♭ Major)**

8 **D HARMONIC MINOR SCALE (Concert F Harmonic Minor)**

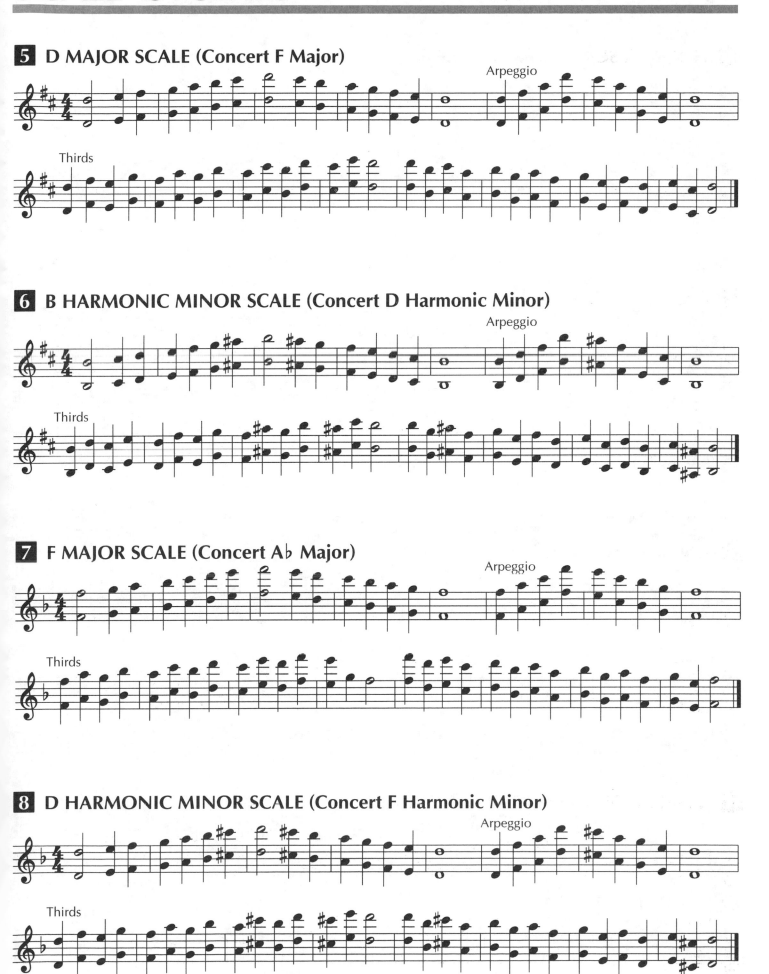

SCALE STUDIES

9 **A MAJOR SCALE (Concert C Major)**

10 **F♯ HARMONIC MINOR SCALE (Concert A Harmonic Minor)**

11 **B♭ MAJOR SCALE (Concert D♭ Major)**

12 **E MAJOR SCALE (Concert G Major)**

13 **CHROMATIC SCALE**

RHYTHM STUDIES

RHYTHM STUDIES

RHYTHM STUDIES

EXCELLERATORS-FOR ALTO SAXOPHONES ONLY

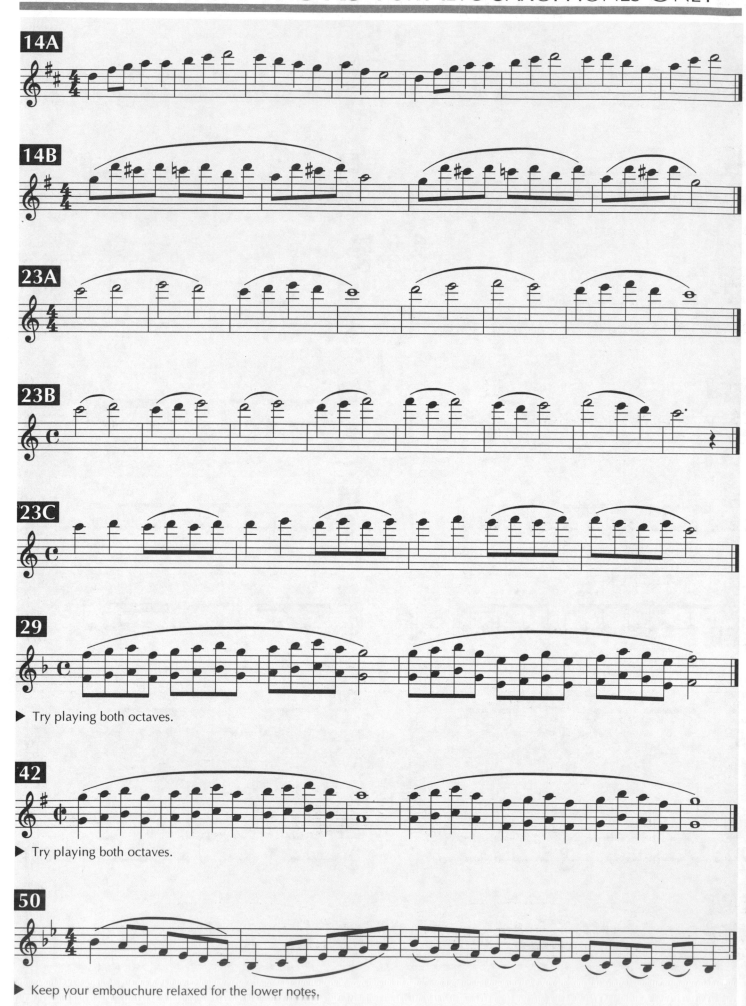

▶ Try playing both octaves.

▶ Try playing both octaves.

▶ Keep your embouchure relaxed for the lower notes.

EXCELLERATORS-For Alto Saxophones Only

▶ *Use the trill fingerings found on page 47.

▶ Slide your right hand little finger when moving from E♭ to C or C to E♭.

Try playing both octaves.

*Use the alternate C fingerings. Try playing both octaves.

EXCELLERATORS-FOR ALTO SAXOPHONES ONLY

119A

▶ * Use the alternate F#/Gb fingering.

119B

▶ * Use the alternate F#/Gb fingering.

121A **B** **C**

124A **B** **C**

▶ Use the [ ] Bb fingering.   ▶ Use the [ ] Bb fingering.   ▶ Use the [ ] Bb fingering.

D **E** **F**

▶ Use the [ ] Bb fingering.   ▶ Use the [ ] Bb fingering.   ▶ Use the [ ] Bb fingering.

125

131

W23XF

E♭ Alto Saxophone Trill Fingering Chart

Move the red key rapidly to produce the trill.
○ = open
● = pressed down

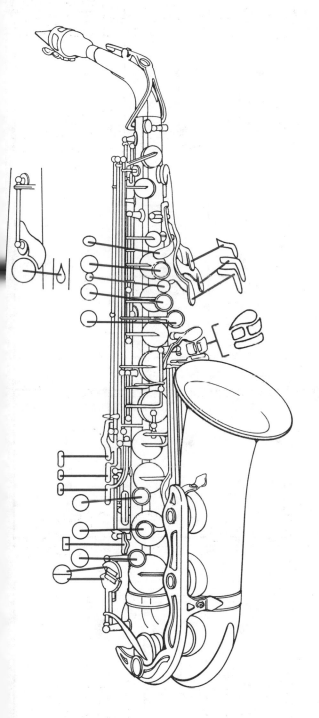

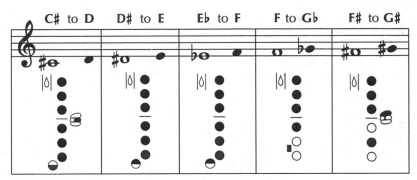

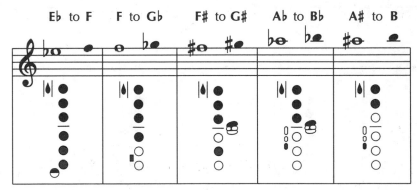

Eb ALTO SAXOPHONE FINGERING CHART

O = open

● = pressed down

When more than one fingering is shown, the first is the most commonly used. Additional fingerings, known as "alternate" fingerings, are used in certain situations to allow for better technique.

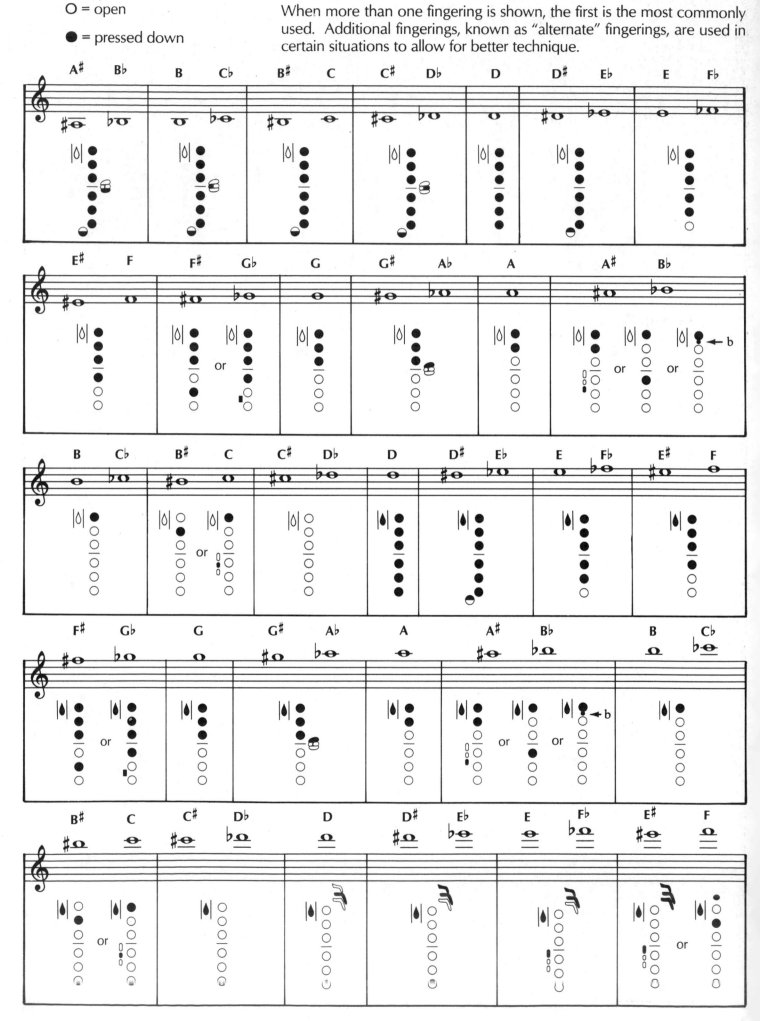